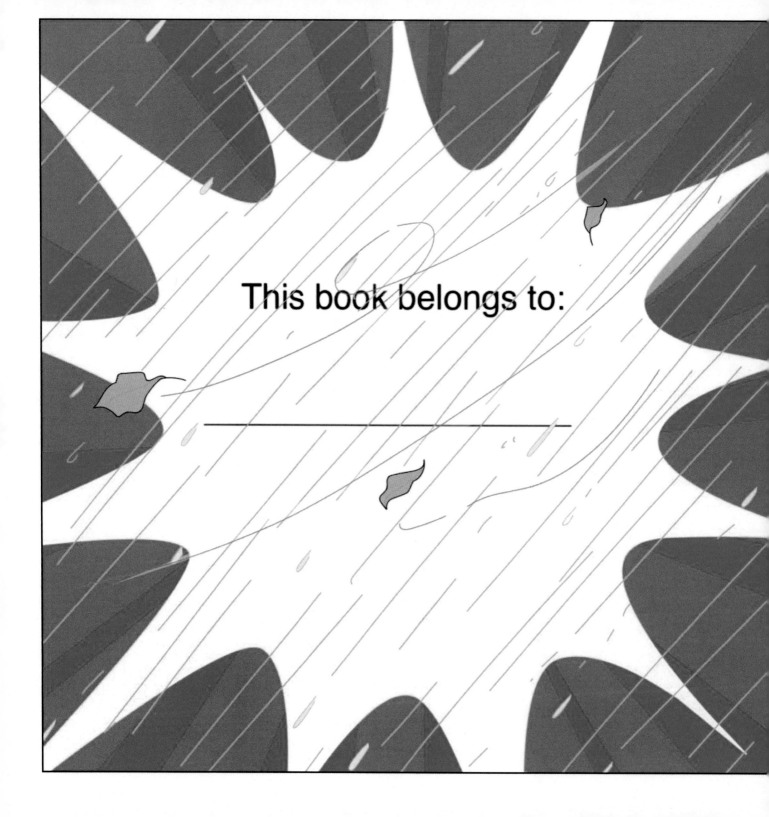

This book belongs to:

_____

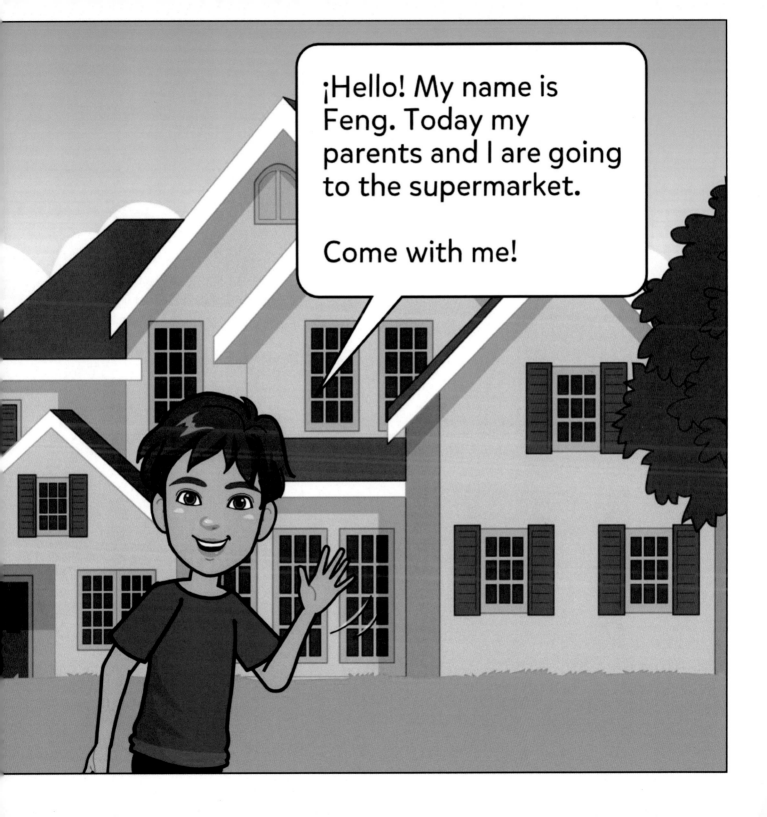

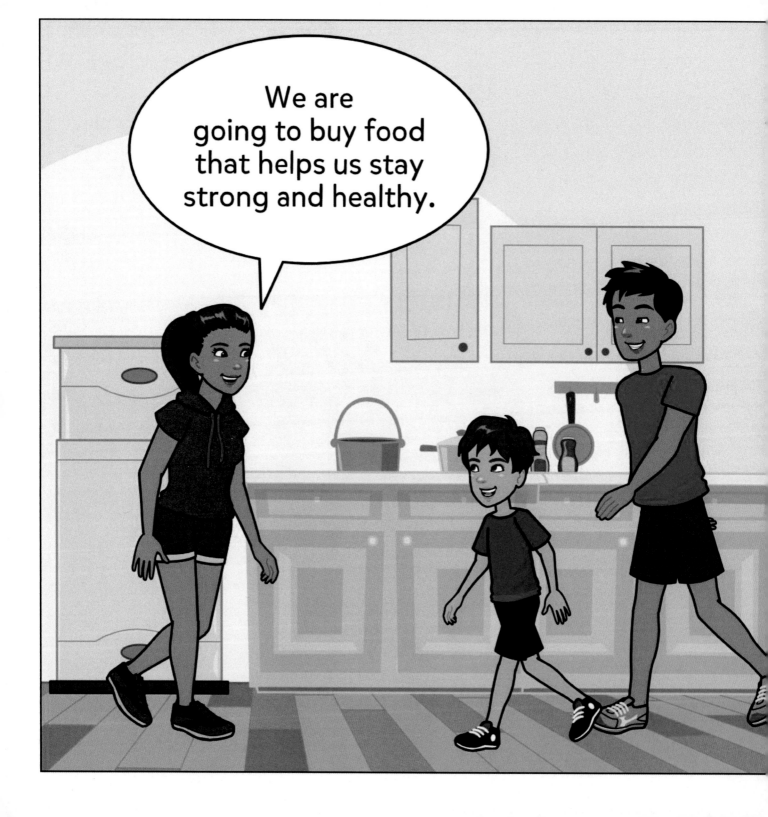

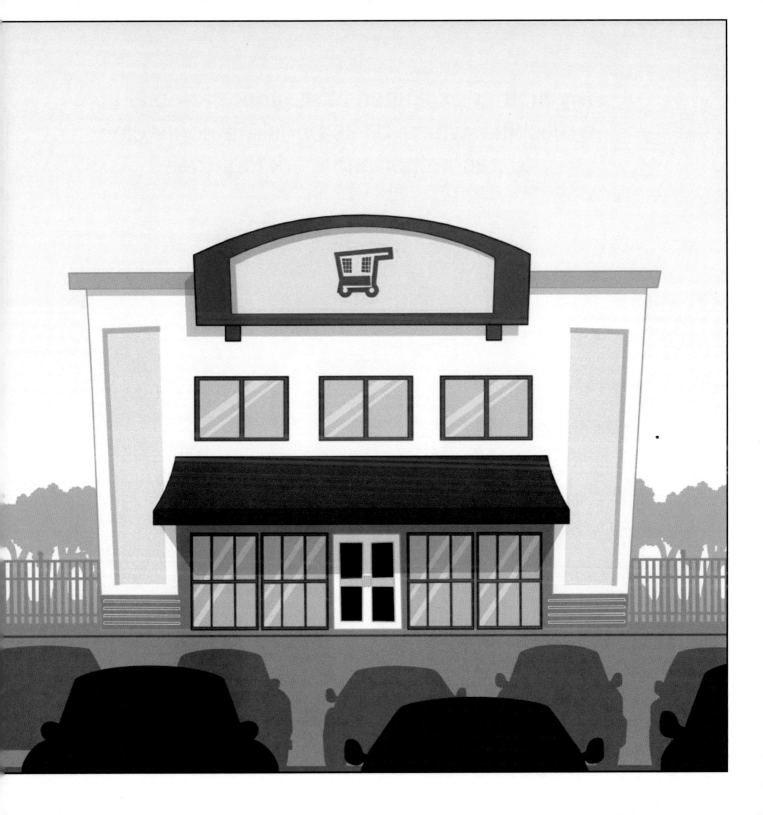

My mother explained to me that our body is
a machine, where all its parts are connected
to each other and work together.

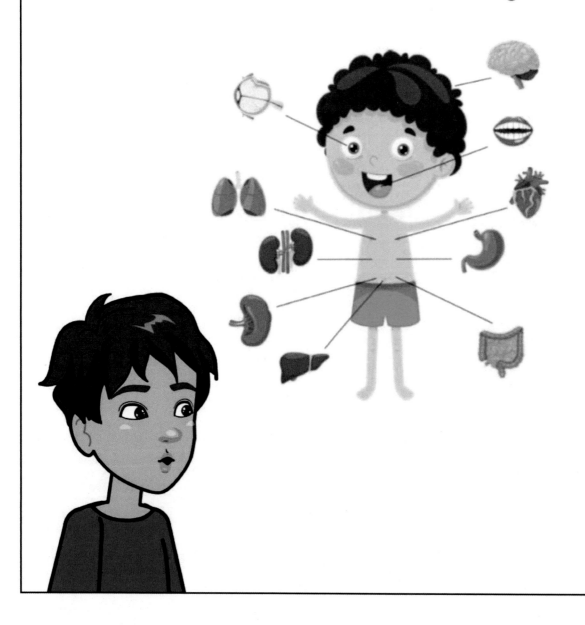

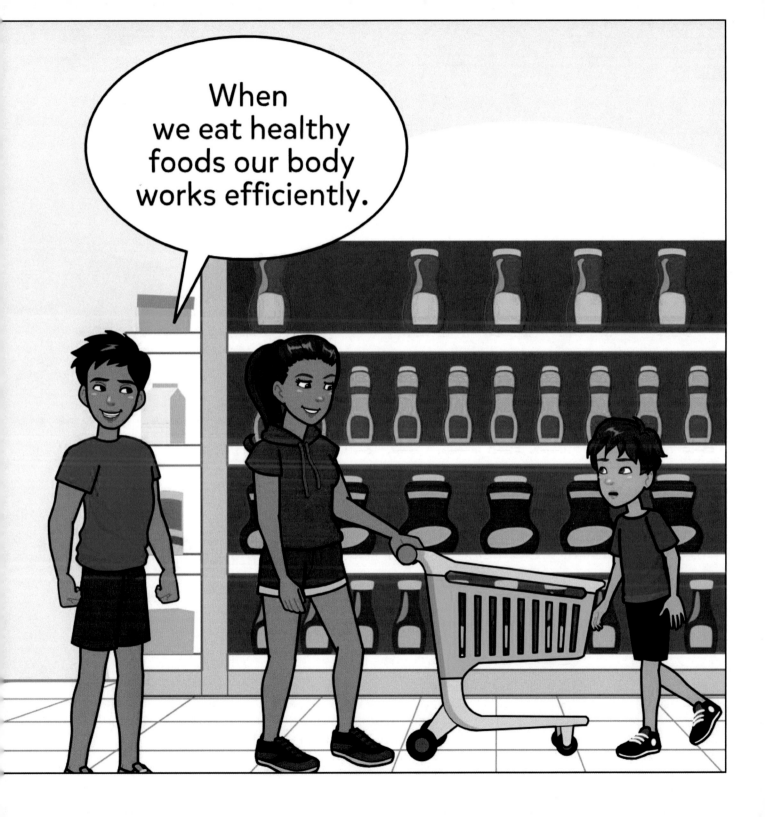

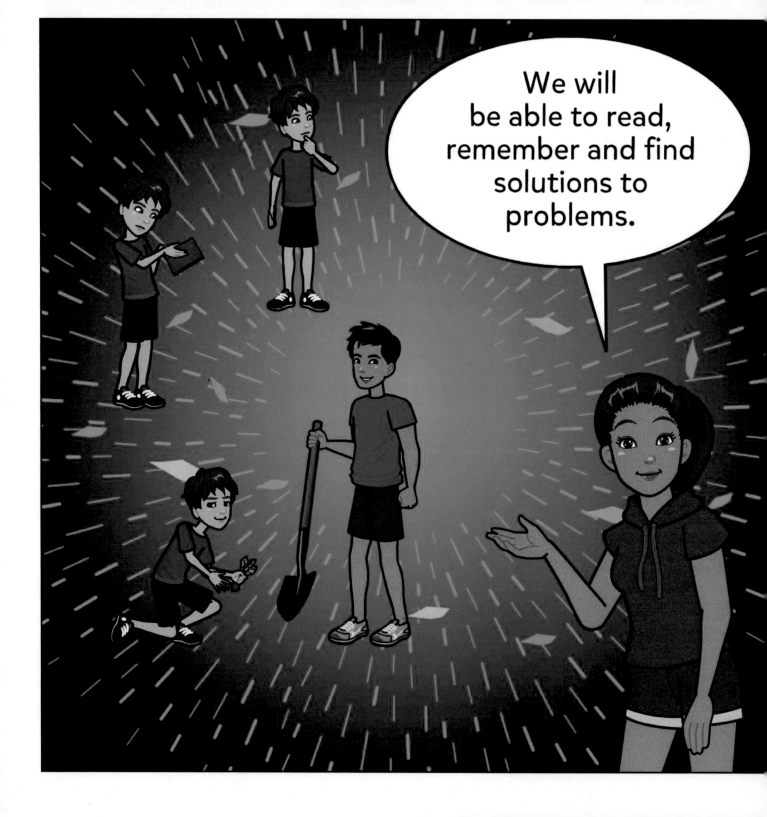

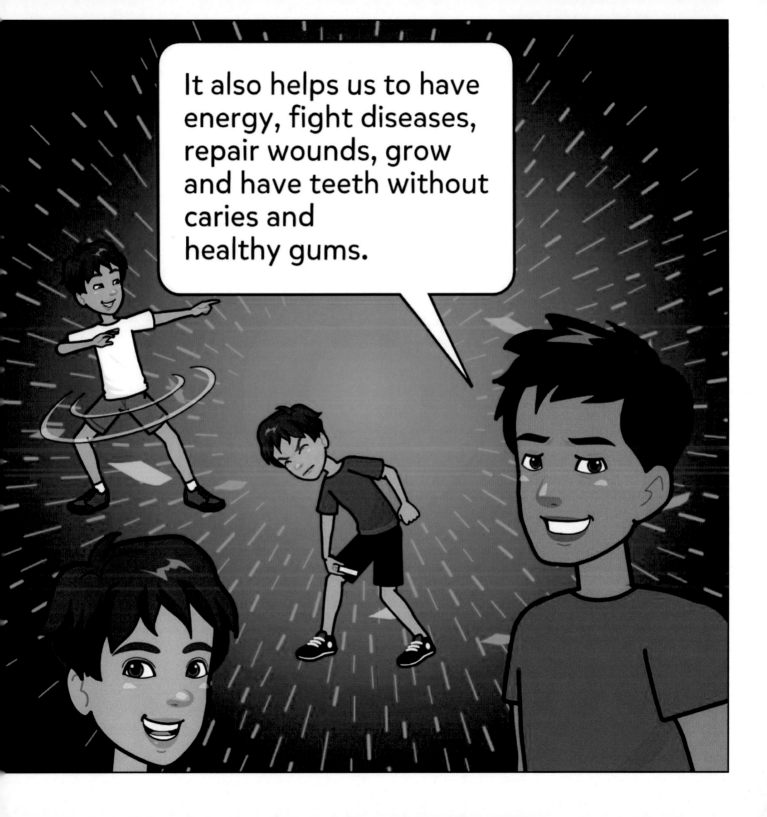

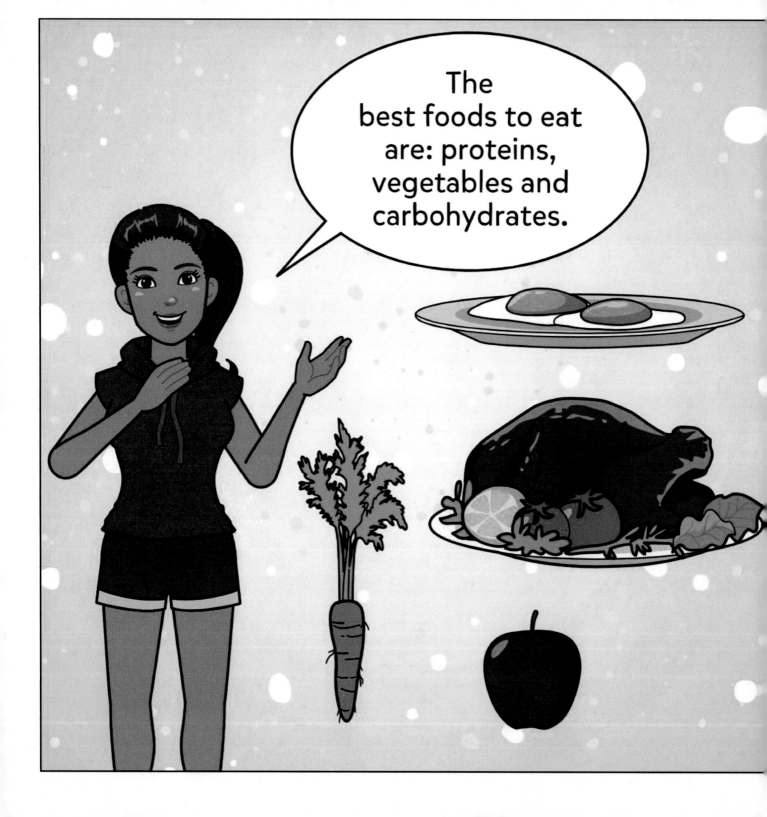

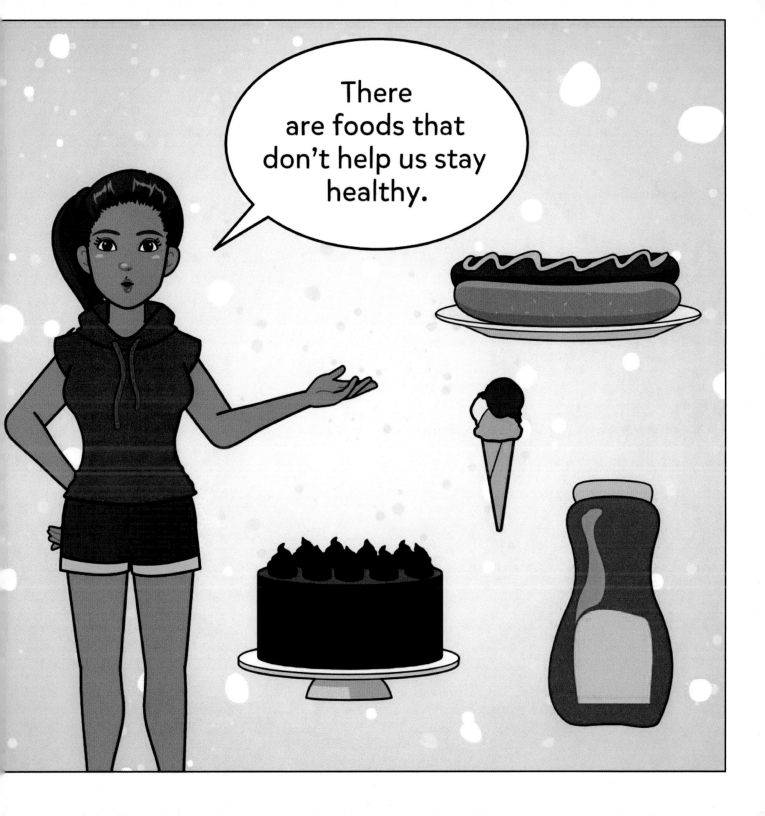

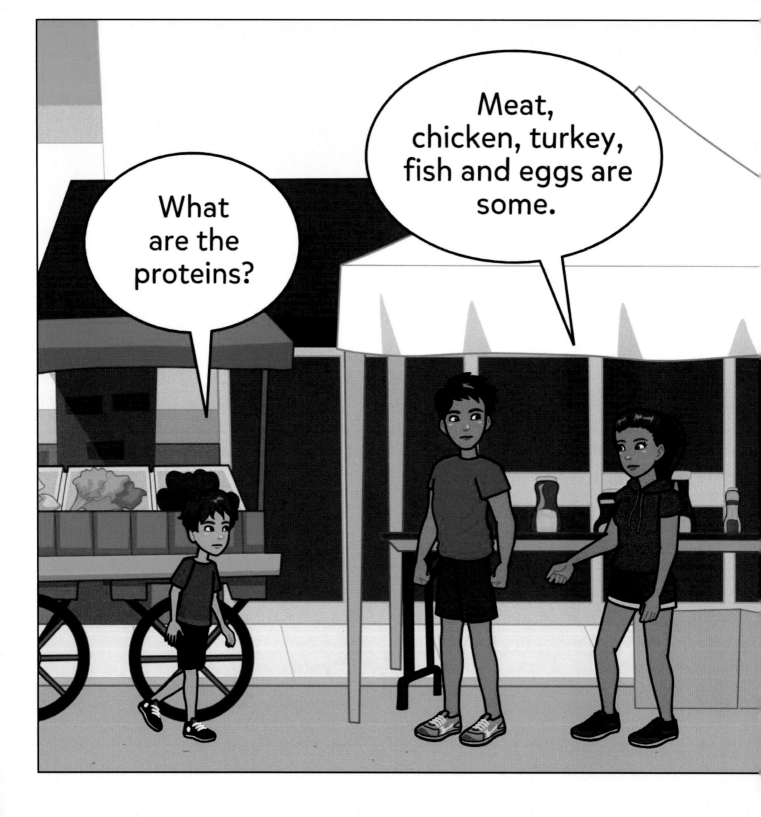

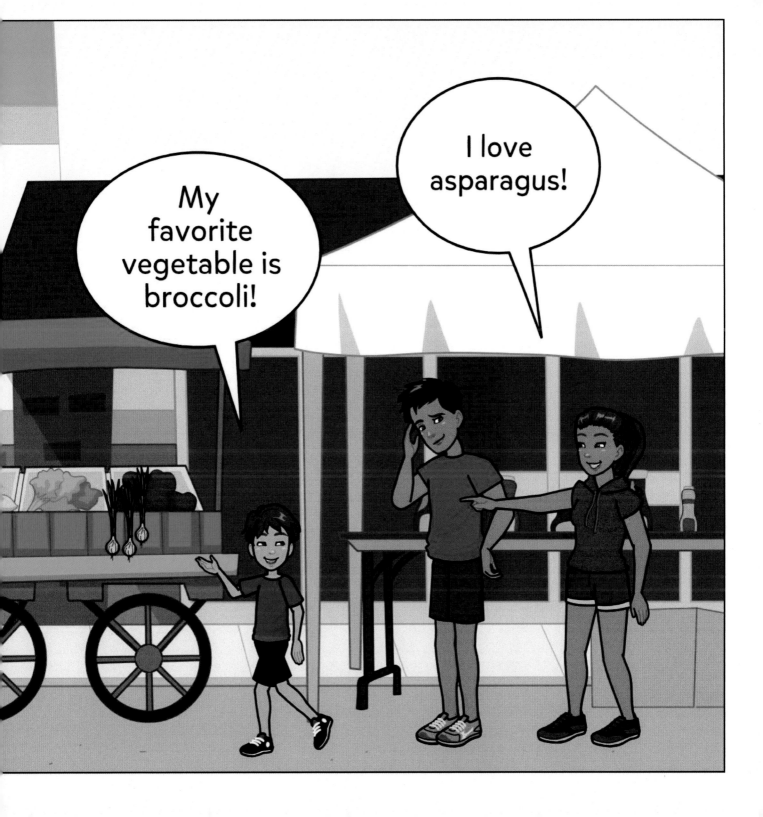

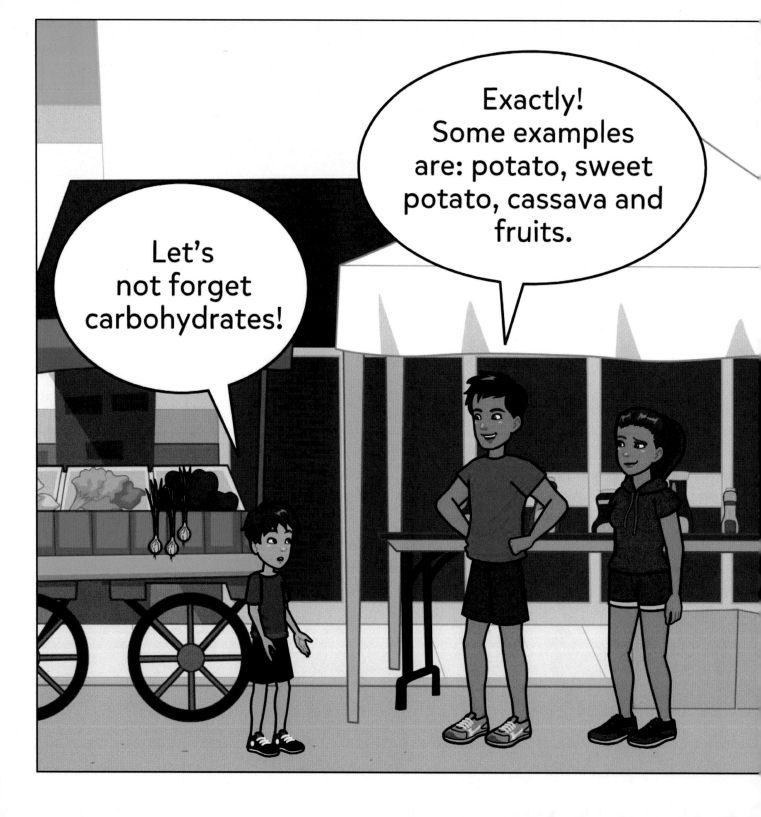

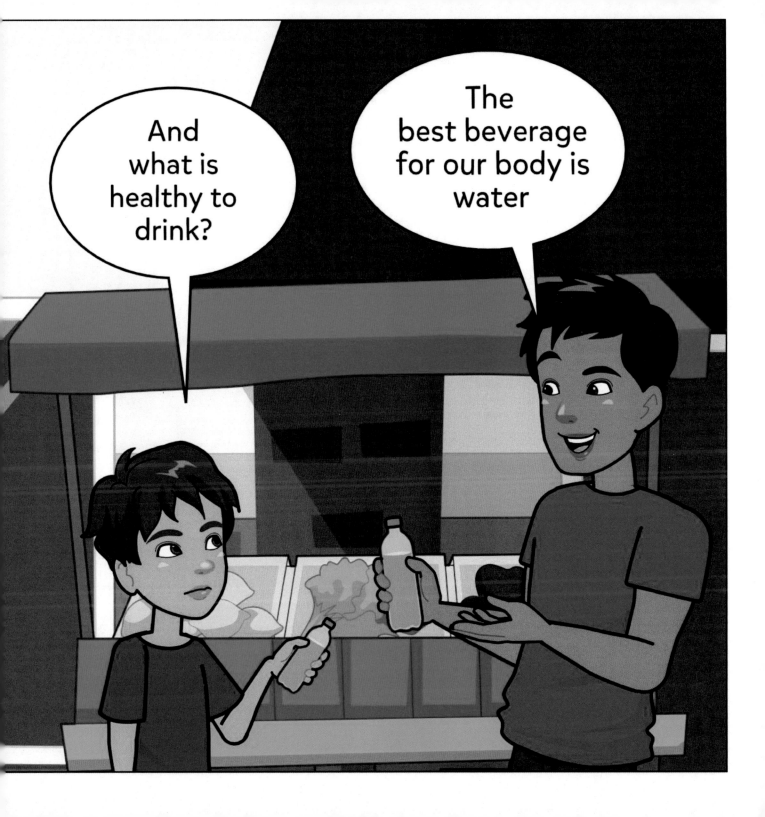

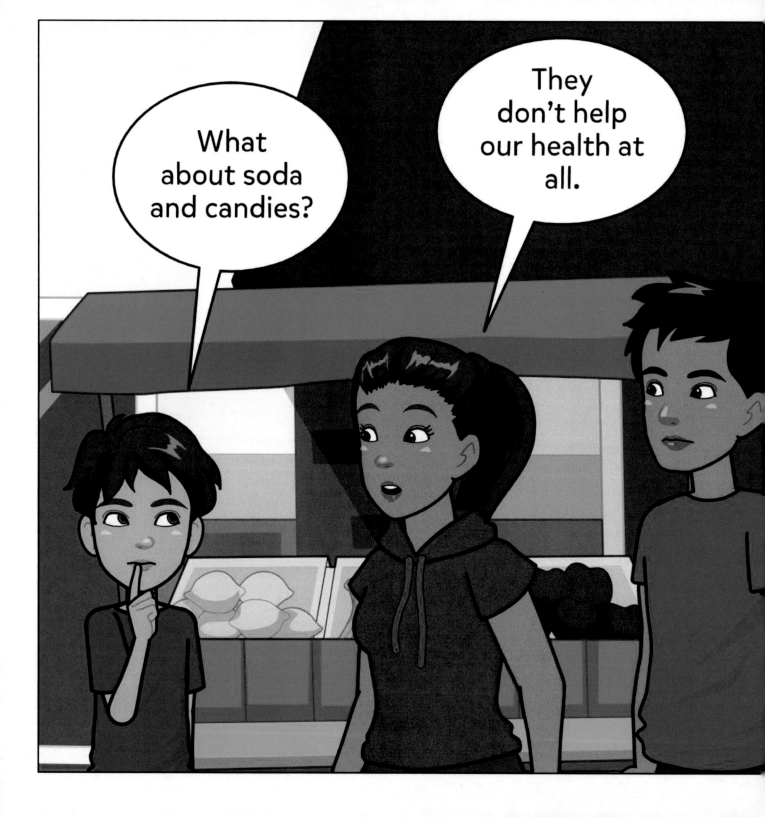

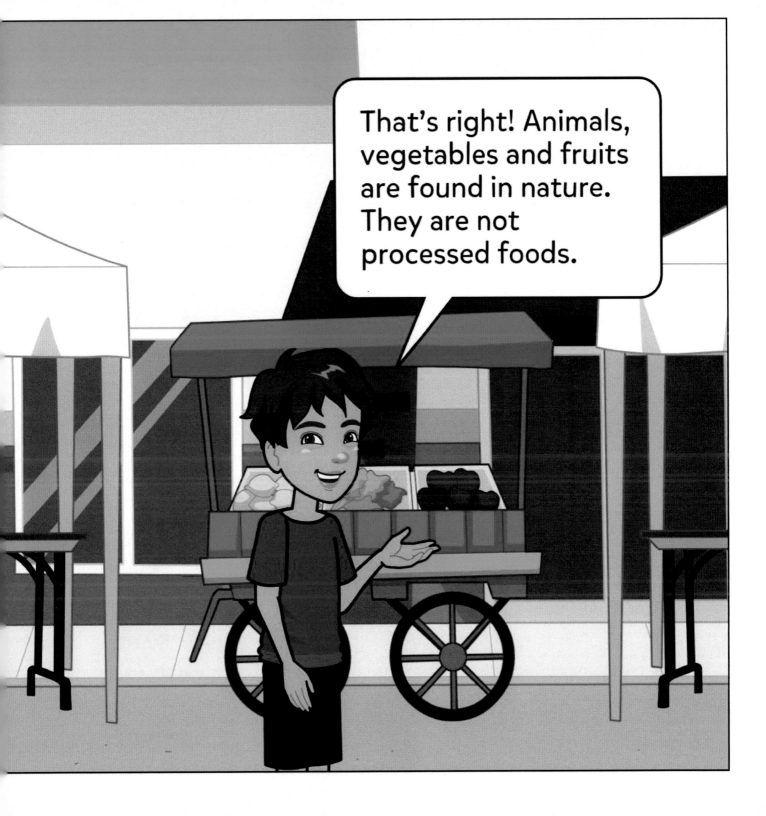

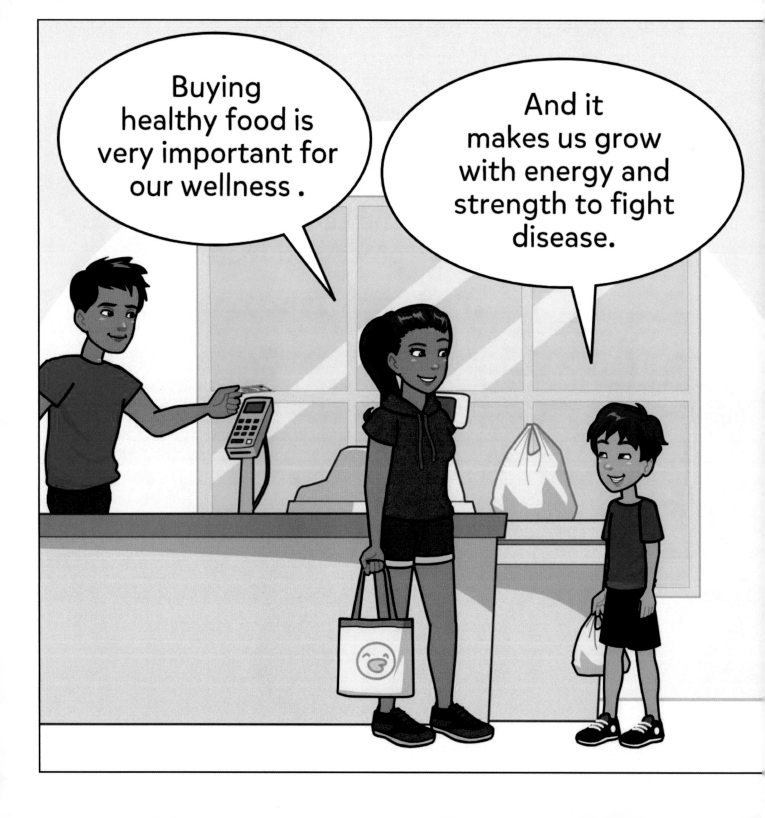

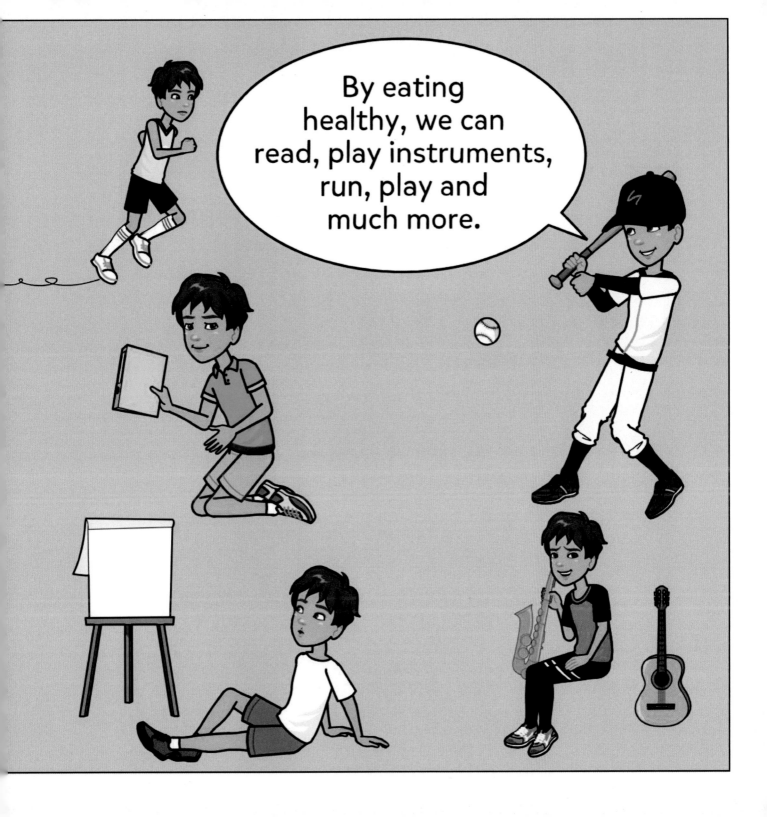

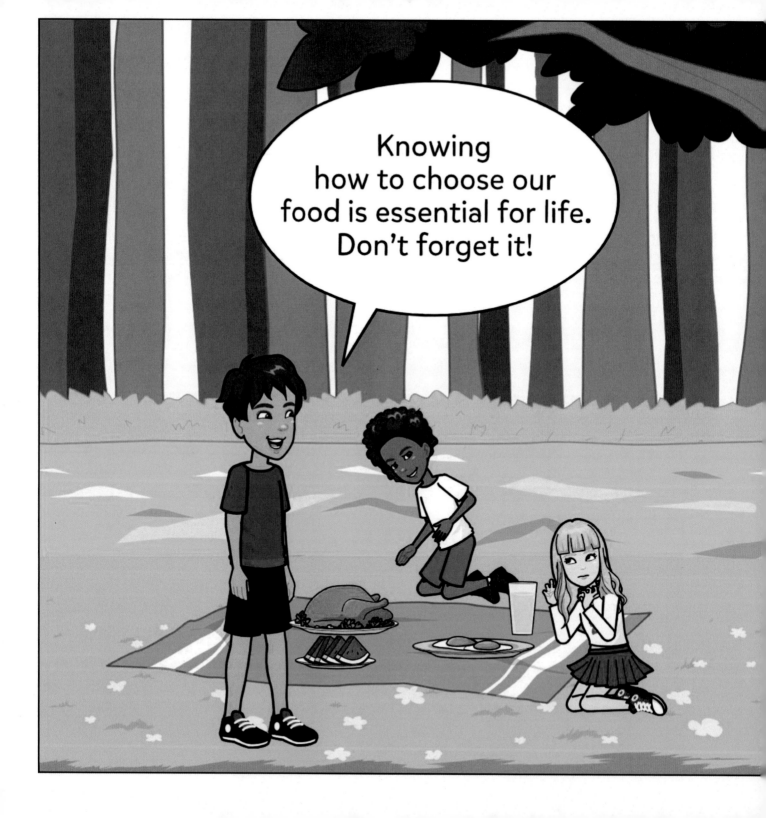

Made in United States
Orlando, FL
15 December 2024